MONSTERS

THE JERSEY DEVIL

BY SHIRLEY RAYE REDMOND

KIDHAVEN PRESS
A part of Gale, Cengage Learning

GALE
CENGAGE Learning™

Detroit • New York • San Francisco • New Haven, Conn • Waterville, Maine • London

© 2009 Gale, Cengage Learning

Every effort has been made to trace the owners of copyrighted material.

LIBRARY OF CONGRESS CATALOGING-IN-PUBLICATION DATA

Redmond, Shirley-Raye, 1955-
 The Jersey devil / by Shirley Raye Redmond.
   p. cm. — (Monsters)
 Includes bibliographical references and index.
 ISBN 978-0-7377-4407-1 (hardcover)
 1. Tales—New Jersey. 2. Devil--Juvenile literature. I. Title.
 GR110.N2R44 2009
 398.209749—dc22

                                                                    2008052914

KidHaven Press
27500 Drake Rd.
Farmington Hills, MI 48331

ISBN-13: 978-0-7377-4407-1
ISBN-10: 0-7377-4407-3

Printed in the United States of America
2 3 4 5 6 7 13 12 11 10 09

Printed by Bang Printing, Brainerd, MN, 2nd Ptg., 11/2009

CONTENTS

CHAPTER 1

SOMETHING IN THE WOODS

For nearly 300 years, residents of New Jersey have told fantastic tales about a mysterious creature supposedly living in the state's Pine Barrens forest. The creature has the head of a dog, the face of a horse, the body of a kangaroo and the wings of a large bat—or so they say. Millions of Americans have never even heard of the Jersey Devil. However since colonial times, this beast has been blamed for crop failure, drought, and the disappearance of livestock.

It is said that the Jersey Devil causes cows to quit giving milk and fish to die in boiling streams. The

This drawing shows what the Jersey Devil supposedly looks like.

creature's terrifying screech is often heard piercing the night. Some say its appearance predicts disaster and war. Interestingly enough, the Jersey Devil was sighted on December 7, 1941—the same day the Japanese bombed Pearl Harbor.

For centuries, parents have told their naughty children that if they do not behave, the Jersey Devil would come out of the woods and take them away. Yet, the hoards of vacationers driving through New Jersey each summer on their way to the beach do not know about the beast that is said to haunt the Pine Barrens. This area of land sprawls across parts of eight counties in south Jersey and covers nearly 2,000 square miles (5,180sqkm) of wooded territory. Every year, terrified campers report nightmarish sounds coming from the woods or the ear-piercing cries of an animal in pain.

Origins

According to legend, the Jersey Devil is the **deformed** offspring born to Mrs. Leeds in 1735 in Leeds Point, New Jersey. Others say that a woman named Mrs. Shourds was the unfortunate mother. Some say the mother of the creature was a young girl in south Jersey, who refused to give food to a hungry gypsy. The gypsy cursed her. Years later, when the girl married, she gave birth to a horribly disfigured child who came to be known as the Jersey Devil. There also is a story that says the Devil is the deformed child of an American colonial

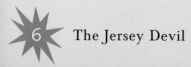

The best-known versions of the Jersey Devil legend blame its horrible appearance and character on some moral failing of the human mother who gave birth to it.

woman and a British soldier. The baby was born disfigured as punishment for the mother's treason. There are many versions of the tale.

One of the most popular tales tells how poor Mrs. Leeds, already the **weary** mother of twelve children, cried out with despair when she found out she was expecting another. Some say she declared she was tired of children and hoped it was a devil.

And according to legend it was! The deformed child was born in a backroom by candlelight during a thunderstorm. Instead of hands and feet, the child had hooves. Instead of a chubby baby face, the monster had a long, bony horse head. Soon the child took on a **fiendish** personality. The horrified Mrs. Leeds kept it locked up in the attic for years. On the night she died, the creature escaped through the chimney. With a flap of its wings and an ear-piercing shriek that shattered the stillness of the night, it was gone.

Something Creepy

Descriptions of the Jersey Devil vary. Some eyewitnesses insist that the Devil is at least 11 feet (3m) tall, with the head of a horse or ram. Others say it's only 3 feet (1m) tall, with the head of a dog and the skin of an alligator around its torso or middle. Nearly all agree that the beast has horns and wings, and a long, forked or pointed tail and dark hair. This odd animal **conglomerate** also is said to have a body like a kangaroo. Its forelegs are short and have claws or birdlike talons. The hind legs are longer, with hooves like a pony or deer. According to some eyewitnesses, the beast is a **biped**, able to run quickly on its hind legs. Some say it spits glowing flames from its mouth in self-defense, like a fire-breathing dragon, and that it stinks.

The Devil's eyes glow red or a bright, greenish-yellow in the dark. They can paralyze any person who stares into them. Its shriek is a high scream that sounds frighteningly human. Others who have heard it say the cry has a high, scratchy sound that ends with a low, rough whisper or hiss. There are those who have described it as a weird combination of sounds, such as the snarl of a hyena and the hoot of an owl. The Devil is nocturnal, meaning it is active at night. It lurks in dark and lonely places, like pine forests, and is said to be able to fly great distances. It has sometimes been heard stamping

Although descriptions of the Jersey Devil's appearance vary, most accounts agree that it has horns and wings, a long-tipped tail, and dark hair.

The Jersey Devil

its hooves on a rooftop. The Devil is known to peek into windows. In December 1993, a New Jersey park ranger named John Irwin reported that a 6-foot-tall (1.8m) biped with black fur suddenly stepped out in front of his vehicle as he drove through the Wharton State Forest. The shaken ranger later reported that the creature also had red piercing eyes and the head of a deer. Was it the Jersey Devil? No one knows for sure.

ON THE RAMPAGE

According to the earliest legends told about it, the Jersey Devil is a fierce, meat-eating monster. Some even say it ate the entire Leeds family before it escaped up the chimney all those years ago. Others say that after escaping through the chimney, it went on a hungry **rampage**, eating several sleeping children in the town.

In 1840 when farmers in the pine woods of New Jersey suffered heavy losses of sheep and chickens, they blamed the Jersey Devil, but they had no proof. Interestingly enough, there is no evidence that the Jersey Devil has ever attacked a human being either, just stories. There are those who insist it has blasted off the tops of trees and danced on fence rails. Some say it occasionally eats cats and dogs and leftovers that it finds in trashcans. Others tell stories about how it eats fish that it catches after breathing hot, burning air over the surface of a lake or pond. However, no one has ever witnessed a

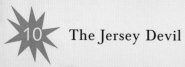
The Jersey Devil

Nineteenth-century New Jersey farmers blamed the Jersey Devil for losses of sheep and chickens.

Devil attack that we know of—except once.

On a cold winter evening in 1909, Mrs. Mary Sorbinski of Camden, New Jersey, heard her dog make a frightened yelp in the backyard. She stepped outside to see what was the matter and was horrified to spy a winged creature clutching her pet in a hard grip. Mrs. Sorbinski tried to save her dog. She made a swat at the monster with her broom. It hooted and hissed at her before releasing the dog and flying away. Shocked and sobbing hysterically, Mrs. Sorbinski carried her injured dog into the house.

The uproar brought her neighbors, who witnessed the dog's injuries. They called the police. A concerned crowd of nearly 100 people gathered in the street in front of the house. When they heard a shrill, high-pitched scream, they were terrified. The police officers rushed up the street to investigate and the group closely followed. Sighting the Devil overhead, they shot at it several times until their weapons were empty. The Devil, apparently unharmed, flew off and disappeared into the night.

CHAPTER 2.

INCREDIBLE SIGHTINGS

Although not widespread, sightings of the Jersey Devil have been reported off and on over the years. Many, of course, are simply tall tales that have been passed down from one generation to the next. Most people do not believe in the existence of the Devil. They insist it is nothing more than an interesting bit of colonial folklore. However, there have been strange reports from believable witnesses that are hard to explain. Whatever it is—or is not—there is or was *something* in the woods.

THE COMMODORE AND THE KING

One of the most famous eyewitnesses was Com-

Commodore Stephen Decatur is one of the most famous eyewitnesses to the Jersey Devil.

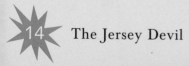 The Jersey Devil

modore Stephen Decatur (1779–1820). He was an American naval hero famous for his sea battles with the Barbary pirates in the early 1800s and for his heroism during the War of 1812 (1812–14). He is the youngest man to ever achieve the rank of captain in the history of the U.S. Navy. Decatur was appointed naval commissioner in 1816 and was responsible for outfitting the nation's warships.

Decatur took his duties seriously. He traveled to the Hanover Iron Works in New Jersey to see how cannonballs were manufactured. Decatur was on the firing range inspecting cannons when, suddenly, there was a bloodcurdling screech overhead. He and the other men were stunned by the appearance of a large, bizarre creature that flapped its way across the firing range. The quick-thinking naval hero fired a loaded cannon. The cannon ball tore a gaping hole in the monster's wing, but the wound did not prevent it from flying away. When Decatur demanded to know what the creature was, the startled witnesses on the firing range told him it must be the Jersey Devil.

Joseph Bonaparte was another famous eyewitness. He was once the unpopular king of Spain, appointed to the throne by his younger brother, French emperor Napoleon Bonaparte. When Napoleon lost power, his brother Joseph gave up the throne of Spain. He moved to the United States and built an estate in Bordentown, New Jersey, on 800 acres (324ha) of land. He lived there from 1816 to 1839 and spent his leisure time hunting and entertaining famous Americans, such as former president John Adams and **orator** Daniel Webster.

One day, while out with his hunting rifle, Bonaparte discovered the footprints of what appeared to be a two-footed donkey. He followed the odd footprints until they disappeared. Then he heard a strange hissing noise behind him. He turned slowly and came face to face with the strangest creature he had ever seen in his life. It towered over him, standing on two feet. It had a head like a horse and large wings. Bonaparte froze and forgot about his rifle. The beast hissed again and then flew away. Later that day, when he mentioned the incident to a friend, he was told he had seen the Jersey Devil. From that day on, Joseph Bonaparte always kept his eye out for the strange creature, but he never saw it again.

Terror in 1909

In the middle to late 1800s there were few believable reports about the Jersey Devil. Folklorist Charles B. Skinner in his book, *American Myths and Legends* wrote in 1900: "It is said that its life has nearly run its course, and with the **advent** of the new century many worshipful commoners of Jersey dismissed, for good and all, the fear of the monster from their mind."[1] All that changed during one terrifying week in January 1909. During that time, thousands of frightened people claimed to see the devil or its footprints, including Mary Sorbinski and her frightened neighbors. Whole communities became hysterical with fear. Factories, schools, and theaters were closed. Armed men rode with shotguns on public transportation to protect passengers.

One of the first sightings to set off the panic took place in the early hours of the morning on Sunday, January 17. Postmaster E.W. Minister of Bristol, Pennsylvania, saw a glowing monster flying overhead. He said it had a ram's head with curly horns and long, thin wings. Its front legs were shorter than its hind legs, and its screech was like a squawk and a whistle at the same time. Two other men, including a police officer, also saw the creature. The officer fired at it. The beast flew away unharmed.

The next day, another police officer—this one in Burlington, New Jersey—spotted a "flying jabberwok with glowing eyes."[2] Soon residents in the area were reporting bizarre footprints in the snow around their homes. One woman saw the Devil lurking in an alley. Another woman, Mrs. Davis White, discovered it in her backyard in Philadelphia. Her terrified screams brought her husband running to her aid. He chased the beast down the street, where it was nearly hit by a trolley car.

In nearby Gloucester City, Nelson Evans reported being awakened by a ruckus in his backyard.

It was about three feet and a half high, with a head like a collie dog and a face like a horse. It had a long neck, wings about two feet long, and its back legs were like those of a crane, and it had horse's hoofs. It walked on its back legs and held up two short front legs with paws on them. It didn't use the front legs at all while we were watching. My wife and

In 1909, as the public hysteria about the Jersey Devil escalated, some communities formed groups to hunt the creature down.

I were scared, I tell you, but I managed to open the window and say, "Shoo!" and it turned around, barked at me, and flew away.[3]

As newspapers a-cross the country eagerly reported these unbelievable sightings, the hysteria in New Jersey and Pennsylvania grew. Businesses and schools were closed. Groups formed to hunt down the monster. Then on the evening of January 21, 1909, the Devil was spotted on a rooftop in West Collingswood, New Jersey. Firemen called to the scene blasted the monster with a stream of water. Enraged, the beast swooped down on them. The frightened firemen fled, and the Devil disappeared.

MORE RECENT SIGHTINGS

Of course, the Devil did not disappear all together. There were occasional sightings off and on over the years. In 1951 several cats, dogs, and chickens were attacked and mutilated. The angry residents

of Gibbstown, New Jersey, blamed the Devil. That same year, a ten-year-old Gibbstown boy claimed that he collapsed after seeing the horrible creature. According to the local newspaper report, the boy declared that the beast had "blood coming out of

Pine Barrens, New Jersey is a place where recent sightings of the Jersey Devil have been declared to be hoaxes.

its face." The boy "began screaming and fell to the floor, his body **wracked** by spasms. The police were called and they searched the area without finding a trace of the ghastly **interloper**."[4]

Soon the rumor that the Devil had returned made its way throughout the county.

A group of teenagers went to the woods to search for the creature. They reported hearing unearthly, bloodcurdling screams. Curious tourists poured into town, hoping to catch a glimpse of the legendary beast. The police chief, tired of endless phone calls, posted signs around town declaring that the Jersey Devil was only a hoax.

Indeed, that is the conclusion that most people have come to in recent years. The Jersey Devil is a hoax—nothing more than a long-lived folk story, meant as a joke. And yet, there continue to be unexplained incidents and sightings that have made even the skeptics sit up and take notice.

In April 1966, for instance, Steven Silkotch blamed the Devil for the slaughter of his entire shed of poultry. Normally, the police and the press would have ignored such accusations. However, when the state troopers arrived to investigate, they discovered not only the mauled remains of chickens, geese, and ducks, but the carcasses of four cats and two large dogs. One of them, a 90-pound (41-kg) German shepherd, had been dragged nearly a quarter of a mile from the attack scene. The dog's thick collar had been chewed to bits. The troopers

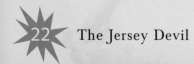

also found strange footprints in the mud. Had they been made by a bear or wildcat? Maybe by an extraordinarily large raccoon? The troopers did not know.

CHAPTER 3

ON THE DEVIL'S TRAIL

The Jersey Devil is a part of New Jersey's state history, culture, and folklore. But does it really exist? Some say, "Absolutely not!" Others are not so sure. There are those who say the Devil once lived in the Pine Barrens, but has since died. Others have wondered if the Jersey Devil is a real demon, with wings and frightening features like a **gargoyle**. Others suggest it is a dragon. To this day, no one has been able to offer a definite explanation for the stories of the Jersey Devil. The many tales about it and the unexplained sightings continue to add to the creature's mystery.

Perhaps the legend is based on nothing more than a case of mistaken identity: an unkempt hermit with long scraggly hair, who startled unsuspecting hikers. Or a person with physical deformities, who hid out in the Barrens, occasionally stealing chickens for food and frightening those who caught a glimpse of him peering through their cabin win-

Some people believe that the Jersey Devil is a real demon living in the woods.

· JUGEND ·

„Glühschrat kommt!"

Max Bernuth (Elberfeld)

dows. We may never know the truth behind the legend.

DEVIL, DOG, OR PTERODACTYL?

While most people do not believe in supernatural explanations for the Jersey Devil, there are many who are convinced that it was or is an animal of some kind. The screams some have reported hearing in the Pine Barrens are said to be nothing more than coyotes, red foxes, or bobcats. Some suggest that the eerie cries are those of an Eastern screech owl. However, the legend is a long-standing one and may influence people more than they realize. Some insist they have heard the Devil's unnerving scream, particularly after learning about a disaster or declaration of war. Perhaps they actually heard the cry of a fox or a distant factory whistle, but looking back, they mistakenly decide it was the Jersey Devil.

Darkness and shadows can play tricks on the eyes too. Many people who thought they saw the Devil may have actually seen something quite ordinary. Some suggest that what people saw was a kangaroo that had escaped from the zoo or a dog with rabies, foaming at the mouth, its eyes glowing red in the twilight. It may even be a hybrid creature, an odd-looking cross between two very common animals. One popular theory is that the Devil is a sandhill crane or a great blue heron. Sandhill cranes stand nearly 4 feet (1.2m) tall and have an impressive

One popular theory is that the Jersey Devil is actually a sandhill crane.

80-inch (203cm) wingspan. They once lived in the marshes of New Jersey. Their mating call is a deep, trumpeting sound. They dance, hop, and bounce in an odd way during the mating ritual. They have very long bills and red eyes. When threatened, they can be aggressive.

The hammer-headed fruit bat bears a striking resemblance to sketches of the Jersey Devil. The male hammer-headed fruit bat is nearly 1 foot (0.3m) tall with a wingspan of more than 2 feet (0.6m). It has a long, horse-shaped face with stiff whiskers around the mouth. It makes a loud, harsh honking sound that can be heard at a considerable distance. Its life span is about 30 years. It lives by sucking the juice out of fruit, mainly figs, but there have been reports of fruit bats attacking chickens. It lives in forests, marshes and swamps—in Africa. Could this animal have somehow made it to the Pine Barrens of New Jersey in the United States?

There is even a tongue-in-cheek theory that the Devil was a pterosaur, or flying dinosaur that survived extinction. Could it still be lurking out there in the pine forest, hiding in a limestone cave? No one knows for sure.

Pranks and Hoaxes

Another explanation is that some distressed witnesses reported Devil sightings that were nothing more than practical jokes or hoaxes. Some suggest that the 1909 "scare" was made up to lower real

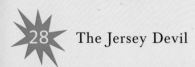

The Jersey Devil

estate prices in the area. Ivan T. Sanderson claimed to have found the fake feet that made the bizarre footprints in the snow. A prankster named G.W.

Some signs of the Jersey Devil, such as strange footprints in the snow, were the work of pranksters.

Green of Salem, New Jersey, admitted many years later that he had made the Devil footprints during that fateful week in January just to keep the hysteria high.

In 1909, when the Philadelphia Zoo offered a $10,000 reward for the capture of the creature, two men named Norman Jefferies and Jacob Hope quickly decided to claim the reward. They borrowed a kangaroo and painted stripes on it. They glued claws and wings to the animal and presented it as the Jersey Devil, "the only rare Australian vampire in captivity." Hope told reporters that the beast was "carnivorous, with a huge appetite, feeding ravenously on rabbits, chickens and other small animals, rending them savagely with its terrible claws. It carried them beneath its bat-like wings until it chose to devour them."[5]

When zoo officials refused to pay the reward, Hope and Jefferies put the odd creature on display, charging 25 cents a person for a glimpse of the painted kangaroo. Years later, Jefferies admitted to participating in the hoax as a publicity stunt to increase **revenues** for the Dime Museum where he worked.

THE HUNT CONTINUES

In 1957 a bizarre corpse was found in the woods. Foresters working for the New Jersey Department of Conservation and Economic Development discovered a partial skeleton, claws, and feathers

on the edge of a cranberry bog. They could not positively identify the charred remains. But some people, hearing of the discovery, insisted it must be the Devil—dead at last. However, sightings have occurred off and on since then, and so the hunt for the Jersey Devil continues.

One group keeps track of all reported sightings on their Web site. They call themselves the Devil Hunters—the Official Researchers of the Jersey Devil. They have no plans to kill the Devil or to capture it. They consider themselves a research team, dedicated to uncovering the truth about New Jersey's most famous **cryptid**. Their first expedition into the woods took place in 1999. The group received national recognition when it was featured

A man participates in a hunt for the Jersey Devil.

on the Fox Family Channel television series, *Scariest Places on Earth* and TLC's *Monster Hunters* series.

The Pinelands Preservation Alliance also sponsors Jersey Devil hunts—just for fun—on several nights in the spring and summer months in the Wharton State Forest. The forest is located in the New Jersey Pinelands National Reserve. Participants gather around a campfire to eat hotdogs and marshmallows, listen to live folk music, and learn the spooky legend of the Jersey Devil of the pines. The three-hour evening program introduces participants to the unique folklore and natural history of the Pinelands. An experienced guide leads the group armed only with flashlights and high hopes. These hunters trek into the woods, listening and watching for the Jersey Devil.

CHAPTER 4

THE JERSEY DEVIL TODAY

Through the years, the legend of the monstrous Jersey Devil has fascinated people on the East Coast. In fact, New Jersey residents have discovered that their special Devil is good for business. It has been depicted on T-shirts, postcards, stationery, coffee mugs, key chains, computer mouse pads, and other souvenirs. Some people sport Jersey Devil tattoos. Singer Bruce Springsteen is nicknamed the Jersey Devil, and there is even a 4x4 Jersey Devil Jeep. The 177th Fighter Wing of the New Jersey Air National Guard Squadron proudly bears the name as well.

The legendary east coast cryptid is a popular subject with science fiction artists and poster illus-

A man displays his tattoo of the Jersey Devil.

trators too. Some depictions are quite scary, such as William Burns' "Conifer Crouser." Burns shows a sinister Jersey Devil lurking in the Pine Barrens, clutching a skull in his talons. Other illustrations are more fanciful, like artist Luc Latulippe's "J is for Jersey Devil." This painting depicts a bright red flying devil that slightly resembles Pegasus, the mythological flying horse.

On the Menu

The Devil has crossed over into many forms of popular culture—even cooking! All sorts of food items have been named in its honor, including the Jersey Devil sundae. This is made using devil's food cake topped with vanilla cream and hot fudge sauce, whipped cream, and a cherry. The Jersey Devil cocktail is an alcoholic beverage made with cranberry juice, apple cider, and brandy. It is garnished or topped with apple slices. There also is a spicy Jersey Devil chili dish and a barbecue sauce.

In Cartoons

The cryptid creature makes appearances in cartoons as well. In the 2007 film called *TMNT* or *Teenage Mutant Ninja Turtles*, Leonardo, Donatello, Raphael, and Michelangelo unite in New York City to fight an army of ancient creatures that threaten to take over the world. One of these monsters is the Jersey Devil. But unlike the legendary Devil,

In the 2007 film TMNT, *the Teenage Mutant Ninja Turtles fight a Jersey Devil that threatens to take over the world.*

this one is portrayed as a small but vicious red devil, with horns and a forked tail. It fights against Raphael in a city diner.

The Jersey Devil even made an appearance on the Disney Channel in the cartoon series *American Dragon: Jake Long.* This show is about a boy with super powers who can turn into a dragon. In the 2005 episode titled "The Long Weekend," Jake goes

camping in the New Jersey woods with his father and best friends Spud and Trixie. There, they meet a community of terrified sprites, or elves, being attacked by the Jersey Devil. Jake turns into a dragon and defeats the Devil, saving the sprites.

The Cartoon Network's *The Real Adventures of Jonny Quest* is an action-adventure cartoon series produced by Hanna-Barbera. In "The Spectre of the Pine Barrens" episode, Jonny, his father Dr. Quest, and the doctor's adopted son Hadji travel to New Jersey to investigate the centuries-old legend.

While there, they become involved in a 200-year-old feud between descendents of the colonial Minutemen and British Redcoats, who are fighting over possession of the original Declaration of Independence. The dreaded phantom of the Pine Barrens helps the Quests bring the feud to an end.

Games, Books and Comics

In 1998 PlayStation released a video game called *Jersey Devil.* This make-believe "devil" is a bat-like superhero who wears a purple mask. After being kidnapped by a mad scientist named Dr. Knarf, he escapes. This devil must later fight the scientist's army of mutant vegetables to keep them from destroying Jersey City.

In 2007 Sterling Publishers released a book for kids who enjoy reading about weird creatures. *The Weird Club, A Search for the Jersey Devil,* written by Randy Fairbanks, is the first in a new series of books for kids. The book is about a boy named Mark who lives in Basking Ridge, New Jersey. Mark wants to organize a Weird Club at school to investigate strange and spooky occurrences. As the title suggests, the club's first investigation involves the Jersey Devil.

The Devil has its own series of comic book adventures too. They were created by Tony DiGerolamo in the early 1990s. In DiGerolamo's version of the legend, the Devil is a mysterious hermit hiding out in the Pine Barrens. His name is J.D. Popular. At comic conventions, these illustrated tales are complicated retellings of Jersey Devil myth and lore, combined with pirate stories and Native American legends.

THE DEVIL ON ICE

The Devil has made a name for itself in sports too. Newark, New Jersey, has been the home of the New Jersey Devils hockey team since 1982. The team is a member of the National Hockey League. Local newspapers sponsored a contest to come up

The New Jersey Devils mascot entertains hockey fans during a game.

with the best name for the team. More than 10,000 people voted to name the players after the strange creature that haunts the Pine Barrens. The current mascot for the team is, of course, a 7-foot (2.1m) devil on ice skates. He keeps the fans excited during the games and entertains during half time.

For more than 300 years, the Jersey Devil has captured the imagination of people on the East Coast. It continues to do so in restaurant menus, cartoons, books, and comics. But watch out! There really could be something mysterious lurking in the vast pine forests of New Jersey—and it flies!

NOTES

Chapter 2: Incredible Sightings

1. Quoted in James F. McCloy and Ray Miller, *The Jersey Devil*. Moorestown, NJ: Middle Atlantic Press, 1976, p. 35.
2. Quoted in Jerome Clark, *Unexplained!* Canton, MI: Visible Ink Press, 1999, p. 562.
3. Quoted in Clark, *Unexplained*, p. 564.
4. Quoted in McCloy and Miller, *The Jersey Devil*, p. 91.

Chapter 3: On the Devil's Trail

5. Quoted in McCloy and Miller, *The Jersey Devil*, p. 89.

Glossary

advent: Beginning or start.

biped: A creature that walks on two legs.

conglomerate: Made up of many different parts from various sources.

cryptid: An unknown or mythical creature.

deformed: Misshapen or warped.

fiendish: Demonic, extremely cruel or evil.

gargoyle: A roof spout or figurine in the form of a grotesque or fantastic creature

interloper: Intruder.

orator: A person who delivers speeches or orations.

rampage: A rage that leads to violence and destruction.

revenues: Money received for goods and services.

weary: Tired.

wracked: Shaken.

FOR FURTHER EXPLORATION

BOOKS

Jerome Clark, *Unexplained!* Canton, MI: Visible Ink Press, 1999. A fascinating reference book that compiles the strange and unexplained sightings of savage black dogs, the Loch Ness monster, and other cryptozoological creatures.

George M. Eberhart, *Mysterious Creatures, a Guide to Cryptozoology.* Santa Barbara, CA: ABC-CLIO, 2002. An easy-to-use encyclopedia of facts and folklore about the world's strangest creatures, from A to Z.

Randy Fairbanks, *The Weird Club: The Search for the Jersey Devil.* New York, NY: Sterling Publishing, 2007. The first book in a series for students 8- to 12-years-old about kids looking for local legends about monsters, ghosts, and space aliens.

James F. McCloy and Ray Miller Jr., *Phantom of the Pines.* Moorestown, NJ: Middle Atlantic Press, 1998. A regional classic about the mysterious creature that is said to haunt the sand trails and misty marshes of southern New Jersey.

Web Sites

The Cryptozoologist (www.lorencoleman.com). This site is part of Loren Coleman's International Cryptozoology Museum in Portland, Maine. It provides information about a wide variety of crypto-creatures, such as Big Foot, the Loch Ness Monster, and the Jersey Devil.

The Devil Hunters–Official Researchers of the Jersey Devil (www.njdevilhunters.com). Folklore, recent sightings, and information about the continued search for the cryptid.

The Pinelands Preservation Alliance (www. pinelandsalliance.org). To learn more about attending a Jersey Devil hunt, visit the Web site and click "Adventures."

INDEX

Picture Credits

ABOUT THE AUTHOR

Shirley Raye Redmond is the author of several nonfiction books for children, including *Mermaids*, *Cerberus*, and *Tentacles! Tales of the Giant Squid*. Redmond lives in New Mexico. Visit her Web site at www.readshirleyraye.com.